GERMS
The Library of Disease-Causing Organisms ™

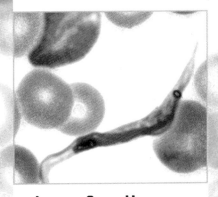

PARASITES

Jennifer Viegas

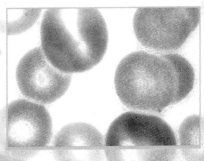

Published in 2004 by The Rosen Publishing Group, Inc.
29 East 21st Street, New York, NY 10010.

Copyright © 2004 by The Rosen Publishing Group, Inc.

First Edition

Library of Congress Cataloging-in-Publication Data

Viegas, Jennifer.
Parasites/Jennifer Viegas.—1st ed.
    p. cm.—(Germs-The library of disease-causing organisms)
Includes bibliographical references and index.
Contents: What is a parasite?—Diseases caused by protozoa and insects—Lice and worms—Understanding and stopping the parasite cycle.
ISBN 0-8239-4494-8 (library binding)
1. Parasitic diseases—Juvenile literature. [1. Parasitic diseases. 2. Diseases. 3. Parasites.]
I. Title. II. Series.
RC119.V54 2004
616.9′6—dc21

                                                    2003009377

Manufactured in the United States of America

On the cover: Electron micrograph of Giardia Lamblia cysts

CONTENTS

1 What Is a Parasite?

All living things, including humans, need other living organisms in order to survive. For almost every creature, this need is fulfilled with food. Humans eat other organisms for food. This is called predation, and humans are predators. Parasites, however, not only feed on other organisms, but they also live in or on them. The ancient Romans first used the word "parasite." It meant, appropriately enough, an unwanted dinner guest.

The animal providing food and shelter for a parasite is called a host. Usually the host is much bigger than the parasite. A larger creature can provide great benefits for a parasite, such as an enormous food supply, tissues that give the parasite protection and warmth, and the mobility to get around and find more hosts.

It is in the best interest of a parasite to keep its host alive, since the host's well-being directly affects the parasite. If the host dies, the parasite might die, too, or at least have to find another host. But parasites are usually fairly simple organisms that act without self-awareness. If they make a host fatally ill, they must move on or die. Many parasites have a complex life cycle that involves moving though several different environments and hosts.

Sometimes the connection between a host and a parasite is an example of symbiosis. The word "symbiosis" means to live together, and in scientific terms it refers to a close relationship between two distinct organisms that benefits both. A colony of ants finds shelter inside a tree. But it also protects the tree from leaf-eating insects. That is a symbiotic relationship. In pure parasitism, though, the host gets nothing from the presence of the parasite.

There are many different kinds of parasites. Some can be viewed only through a microscope. Others can grow to be several feet long. All can be divided into three basic groups: protozoa, worms, and parasitic insects and arachnids.

Protozoa

Microscopic, single-celled organisms are called protozoa. These tiny creatures are neither plant nor animal, but are classified as somewhere in between. The word "protozoan" is derived from the Greek word for "first," *protos*, referring to the fact that these organisms are some of Earth's simplest life forms and were probably among the first living creatures to evolve on the planet.

Not all protozoa are parasites. Many, particularly those that thrive in water, do just fine all on their

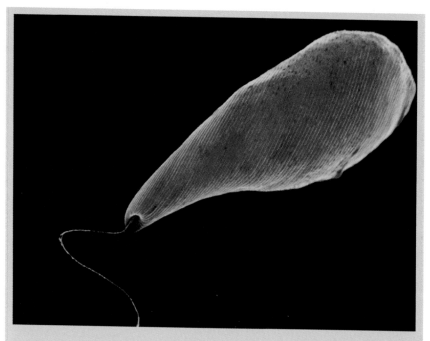

Euglena, seen above, is a flagellate species of microscopic one-celled organisms. They live in fresh water and tend to form a green scum on ponds and drainage ditches in warm weather.

own, as long as they are in the right environment. Amoebas, for example, derive their food and oxygen from the water in which they live. Some protozoa are green in color because, like plants, they have organelles containing chlorophyll, which produces food from sunlight. Still other protozoa do need a host in order to survive, making them parasites.

Protozoa can be divided into four categories: flagellates, sarcodines, apicomplexans, and ciliates. Flagellates possess hairlike appendages that enable them to move quickly and smoothly through water. Many are harmless, but some, like the group called the trypanosomes, can cause disease.

Sarcodines use pseudopods, or "false feet," to move. The pseudopod resembles a miniature toe. Some sarcodines can cause disease when ingested, but many are harmless. One ocean group even grows chalky skeletons that the creatures shed. Over time the skeletons build up and create structures similar to the shells that other animals use for shelter.

Unlike flagellates and sarcodines, all apicomplexans are parasites. They move by gliding through their environment. A number of apicomplexans can be quite dangerous to humans. Malaria, for example, is caused by an apicomplexan parasite.

Ciliates are like flagellates in that they also possess hairy growths on the exterior of their cells to help them move. More developed in structure, however, ciliates are the most complex form of protozoa. They may have other complex anatomical features to help them survive, such as tubes that aid in feeding.

Worms

Worms are animals that possess a soft, thin body without a backbone or limbs. Chances are you have seen worms in your backyard or at a park. That is because worms often live in soil or water. Many are very essential to their environments, serving as clean-up crews and adding beneficial nutrients to the soil. Parasitic worms, on the other hand, can pose a danger to plants, humans, and animals. In the best case, a parasitic worm feeds off of its host without the host even knowing that the worm is present. In the worst case, blood and nutrients can be lost, leading to health disorders.

Worms are divided into four primary groups: flatworms, ribbon worms, roundworms, and segmented worms. Flatworms are indeed flat but come in different shapes. Some are narrow, while others grow in an oval form. Flatworms and other worms that do not live as parasites are free to move about in the soil or water and have a variety of food sources. Parasitic flatworms, like flukes and tapeworms, rely on other creatures for their nourishment. They can pose serious health problems to humans and other animals.

Ribbon worms are like flatworms, only larger. In fact, some ribbon worms can grow to become several feet long. Many are parasitic, feeding on animals such as sea creatures and even other worms.

These *Trichinella spiralis* roundworms can be present in undercooked meat, causing the disease trichinosis in humans. While not usually fatal, trichinosis can lead to digestive and muscle problems.

Roundworms possess long, tubular bodies. This is the largest group of worms, with approximately 12,000 species. Most free-living species inhabiting the water and soil are perfectly harmless. Parasitic roundworms, however, can hurt their hosts by causing disease.

The bodies of segmented worms are divided into sections that look like rings. Again, many are harmless to humans but some, like leeches, feed off the blood of their hosts.

Parasitic Insects and Arachnids

Insects are small, air-breathing animals that are invertebrates, meaning that they do not have backbones. They are usually characterized by six legs and a body divided into three parts. A unique feature is their exoskeleton, a hard shell covering their soft body parts. They may or may not have wings. Arachnids are a type of insect with eight jointed legs and a segmented body.

Why Sharks Tolerate Freeloading Fish

Sharks are one of nature's toughest predators. So why are they often seen accompanied by groups of small fish? Usually these fish are remoras, also known as sharksuckers or suckerfish. These fish possess tiny suction cups on the tops of their heads. Remoras literally attach themselves to the underside or belly of a shark and hitch a free ride. In addition, the remoras gain protection from predators and feed off of scraps that fly from the shark's mouth. In return, it is believed that remoras remove and consume parasites from the shark's body.

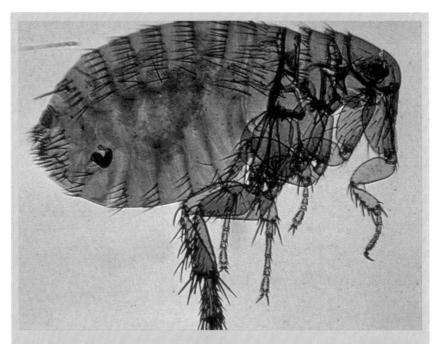

During part of their life cycle, fleas live on the blood of humans and other mammals. While their bites can cause skin irritation and anemia, the bacteria that fleas carry can cause a number of diseases, including typhus and bubonic plague.

The spider is one common arachnid, but the group also includes ticks and mites, which are parasitic.

Except for one species of mite that lays its eggs in human skin, insect parasites and arachnids live on the skin instead of inside the body of their host. Fleas, lice, and ticks are common parasitic insects. They have mouthparts that enable them to attach themselves to the skin where they can draw out nutrients.

While mites, fleas, ticks, and lice tend to target one species as a host, another group of insects, known as blood-sucking micropredators, prefers to take a small amount of blood from a number of different hosts. Biting flies, such as tsetse flies, sand flies, and black flies, are micropredators, along with mosquitoes. Technically they are not parasites, but they can carry protozoan parasites in their bodies and spread disease.

Many insects are free-living for part of their lives and parasitic at other times. For example, fleas begin life in an egg. When hatched, the larvae, which resemble maggots, are not parasites. When the fleas become adults, they become parasites.

Mutualism

Mutualism is a form of symbiosis. It means that both parties benefit from the relationship. One of the most interesting forms of mutualism occurs between a blue-green algae and a fungus. Together they create an entirely new organism known as lichen. The fungus component absorbs and retains moisture. The algae contains chlorophyll and works to create carbohydrates for food. As a team, the association results in a plant that thrives in even inhospitable areas, such as on the surface of rocks.

2 Diseases Caused by Protozoa and Insects

A healthy person is said to be in a state of homeostasis, or stability. Diseases and parasitic organisms can threaten this stability, causing systems within our bodies to become unbalanced and to malfunction. For example, when a person is infected with a flu virus, he or she will experience a higher than normal body temperature. The high temperature is a sign that the immune system is fighting the virus. But if someone's temperature goes too high, it can be life threatening.

Protozoa are different from viruses. Viruses are inert, meaning that they do not have the power to move on their own, an ability that protozoa possess. Parasitic protozoa that cause illness and disease in animals and humans are pathogenic. A pathogenic parasite benefits at the expense of its host.

Each year in the United States, thousands of people become ill as a result of ingesting parasitic protozoa. It is important to remember that protozoa are microscopic creatures, meaning that they can be viewed only under a microscope. Water, food, and soil containing the parasites may not appear to have any outward signs of contamination. Humans

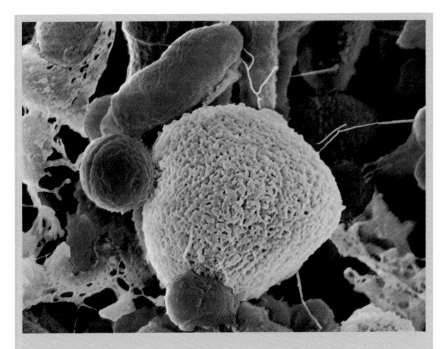

A scanning electron micrograph of the cyst form of *Giardia lamblia*, the protozoa that causes giardiasis. *Giardia* cannot be seen or smelled, which is why inexperienced hikers and campers often catch the disease when they drink stream water that hasn't been boiled or filtered.

usually suffer from protozoan disease after having ingested contaminated water or food. Both of these sources harbor different types of parasites.

Waterborne Parasites

Waterborne disease is still fairly common in the United States, with many states reporting cases of illness each year. Two of the most common diseases caused by protozoa in water are giardiasis (pronounced jee-are-DYE-uh-sis) and cryptosporidiosis (krip-toe-spor-id-ee-OH-sis). Both get their names from the parasitic protozoa that cause the illnesses.

Giardiasis occurs when a person or animal becomes infected with a parasite called *Giardia lamblia*. This parasite can be found in soil, food, and water, and on moist, contaminated surfaces. Ingesting water containing the parasite is a common way in which giardiasis is spread. Frequently, water will contain sewage or feces that harbor the parasites. *Giardia lamblia* is especially hearty and can survive in a dormant state for extended periods of time. That is because the parasite is covered with a protective outer shell. The parasite is impossible to detect in water unless viewed under a microscope.

Symptoms of giardiasis include diarrhea and other intestinal problems, stomach cramps, and sometimes nausea, dehydration, and weight loss. Symptoms usually last anywhere from two to six weeks, but may last longer. Sometimes outbreaks occur after flooding, when sewage or waste runoff enters the water supply. A person can also become infected after swallowing contaminated water found in improperly treated swimming pools, hot tubs, Jacuzzis, and fountains, or in natural settings such as lakes, rivers, springs, ponds, and streams. Giardiasis is usually treatable with prescription drugs.

A tiny parasite called *Cryptosporidium parvum* causes the diarrheal disease cryptosporidiosis, better known as "crypto." Similar to the giardiasis parasite, the crypto parasite possesses a shell that enables it to survive outside of its host or in certain environments for long periods.

Crypto is spread like giardiasis and has similar symptoms. The main difference is that with crypto, the symptoms usually become apparent two to ten days after the victim is infected. The illness may then persist for a couple of weeks, during which time the sick person may go through cycles of feeling better and feeling worse before the illness finally goes away completely.

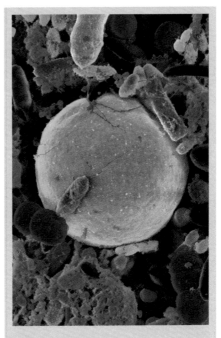

The *Cryptosporidium* parasite can be transmitted from domestic animals to people, causing weakness and diarrhea. The infection is more severe and more common in people with immune-system diseases such as AIDS.

Protozoan Disease in Food

Food, like water, can provide an environment in which parasites can live and wait for a host, such as an unsuspecting hungry human. Two parasitic diseases commonly spread through contaminated food, in addition to water, are amebiasis and cyclospora.

The single-celled parasite called *Entamoeba histolytica* causes the intestinal illness amebiasis

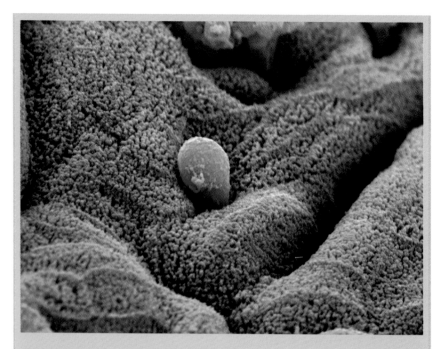

Entamoeba histolytica, shown above, is a species of protozoa that causes amebic dysentery. In most infected humans, the symptoms are intermittent and mild, but in more severe cases, the stomach or intestines can rupture, causing death. Boiling water before drinking it can kill the protozoa. Some research has shown that fresh whole papaya seeds can help prevent dysentery.

(am-e-BYE-a-sis). It is a common disease in developing countries with poor sanitary conditions. Most victims in the United States are recent immigrants, people who have contracted the illness traveling outside of the country, or those who live in poorly maintained housing facilities.

The symptoms of amebiasis are usually mild, but the disease can progress to a severe form called amebic dysentery. With amebic dysentery, the victim may experience severe stomach pain, fever, and even damage to the lungs or brain. The parasite literally invades the body, where it grows and spreads. If left untreated, amebic dysentery can be fatal. People become infected with the parasite after swallowing contaminated food or water, or by touching the cysts, which are the eggs of the parasite, and then accidentally bringing the eggs to the mouth. The cysts, invisible to the naked eye, could be present on surfaces contaminated with the parasite.

Caused by the *Cyclospora cayetanensis* parasite, cyclospora was only first identified in 1979. Since then, outbreaks of the disease have been reported in the United States and Canada. As for most parasitic protozoan diseases, it is spread by drinking contaminated water, by eating contaminated food, or by hand-to-mouth contact after touching a surface with the parasite on it.

It takes days, even weeks, for a person to feel the first symptoms of cyclospora, which causes intestinal problems. That is because the parasite multiplies in the body after passing through the liver. If left untreated, victims of the disease could suffer for a month or longer, during which time there may be periods of feeling better followed by relapses.

How Insects Transmit Disease

Insects and other animals that can spread disease are known as vectors. In virtually all cases, the insects themselves are not harmful unless present in large numbers. They are dangerous to animals and humans because of the parasites, bacteria, and other germs that they might carry and then transfer to bite victims.

Insect vectors for parasitic diseases fall into two groups. The first consists of mosquitoes and other flying, biting insects. These insects usually possess a mouthpart similar to a needle. They puncture the skin of victims and draw out blood. If the insect has parasites in its body, the parasite might spread into the victim's blood or lymphatic system during the bite. Diseases that might not otherwise travel easily from person to person can spread rapidly in the presence of biting insects. A mosquito, for example, might bite an infected person. That mosquito could then bite another person, and then another, spreading the parasitic disease.

Malaria

Worldwide, malaria is one of the most serious and widespread parasitic diseases. It is spread by mosquitoes. It is said that more than 40 percent of the world's population is at risk. In the United States, most cases occur among immigrants and those who travel to areas where malaria is a concern.

Four types of parasites, four different species of plasmodium, an amoeba-like microorganism, can lead to malaria. In each case, the parasites must grow in the mosquito for a week or more before an

At upper left: The blue dots are malaria parasites in a mosquito's stomach. *At center:* An *Anopheles gambiae* mosquito, which is common to Africa and responsible for most of the transmission of malaria, feeds on a human host. *At lower right:* The blood cell marked in green is infected with malaria parasites.

infection can be transmitted to a victim. After a person is infected by the parasites through a mosquito bite, the parasites travel to the liver, where they grow, multiply, and enter the individual's red blood cells, which later burst. Victims feel as though they have a terrible case of the flu. If left untreated without prescription medication, one form of the disease can cause kidney failure and may even result in death. In some cases, the parasites can lay dormant, or remain inactive, in a person's liver for up to four years before the parasites revive, multiply, and cause illness.

Fleas, Ticks and Other Bugs

While mosquitoes themselves are not parasites, fleas and ticks are. As adults, these wingless insects must live on other creatures, such as birds and mammals, including humans, in order to survive. Unlike most mosquitoes, they can pose a health risk even if they are not infected with a parasitic bacteria or germ.

How to Safely Remove a Tick

If you go camping or spend any amount of time outdoors, chances are that you may become a host for a tick. As viruses and bacteria can be present in the tick's body, it is important to remove the tick carefully. This should be done with a pair of fine-tipped tweezers. Grasp the tick closest to the skin and lift it out, being careful not to squeeze the tick's round body. It is a myth that lighting a match or using petroleum jelly will help. They can even do more harm, because if the tick becomes irritated, it may tighten its grip and inject even more potentially dangerous fluid into your body.

Both fleas and ticks feed on blood. They attach themselves to a host and then puncture the skin to draw out the nourishing blood. Because fleas and ticks rapidly multiply, they can weaken the host and cause anemia, an illness that may result from blood loss. The skin will often become inflamed and itchy, as bug mouthparts can become imbedded in the skin.

In terms of disease, fleas and ticks can spread a number of different viruses and bacteria to hosts. Fortunately, most of

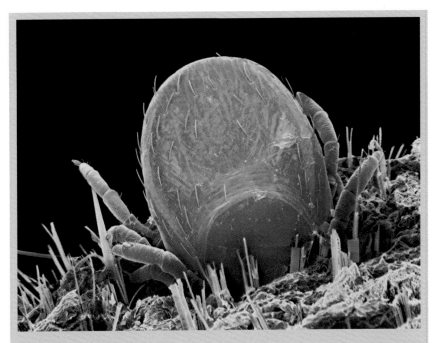

A tick feeds head-down on human skin. Ticks are arachnids, related to spiders. They feed on mammals and birds by cutting through the skin and inserting a feeding tube to collect blood. Ticks can transmit diseases such as relapsing fever and Lyme disease, and tick bites can become infected.

these diseases have been controlled in modern times. In the past, diseases like typhus and plague sickened many people. Plague, caused by the bacterium *Yersina pestis*, which was spread by fleas and the rodents who carried them, caused devastating epidemics in medieval Europe in the fourteenth century.

3 *Lice and Worms*

Lice and certain kinds of worms are parasites. Like parasitic protozoa, insects, and arachnids, these parasites can affect human health. While protozoa are usually invisible to the naked eye, both lice and worms can usually be seen in their adult stages of life because they generally are larger than protozoa. Lice and parasitic worms are not exactly attractive creatures, both in terms of their physical appearance and how they can hurt us, so it pays to take steps to avoid allowing them to choose you as a host.

Lice

The parasitic insect known as a louse is so common that you probably know someone who has suffered from an infestation. Every year, anywhere from 6 to 12 million people contract head lice, a species of lice adapted to living on the human scalp and neck. Many victims are between three and ten years old. That is because children often have little regard for the environment they play in, and so the insects spread very easily.

Lice spread only when there is direct contact with a person who has lice, or with items that may have touched the infected person's hair. These items may include clothing, hats, combs, carpeting, a bed, pillows, a couch, or bath towel. Often, contact occurs during recess, school sports, or even at slumber parties and camping trips.

When lice move into someone's hair, they can go through their entire life cycle right on that person's head. Lice begin as nits, or eggs. The eggs look like yellow or white specks and can be confused with dandruff, or dried skin particles. The eggs attach to the hair shaft where they later hatch.

Upon hatching, the nit becomes a nymph. The nymph is a very small, flat-bodied, wingless insect. It requires blood to survive, so at this stage the lice attach themselves to the scalp and begin to feed. After about seven days, the nymphs mature into adult lice, which look like little

Human lice likely co-evolved with people. Lice are very host-specific; human lice, for instance, will not feed upon other animals, and lice of other animals will rarely feed upon a person.

whitish, six-legged sesame seeds. Lice are so dependent on humans for food and shelter that they will die within a day of falling off the host's head.

Symptoms of lice infestation include itching, a tickling feeling on the head, and visible signs of the parasites themselves. While relatively harmless, lice are hardly welcome guests. They can lead to infections if scratching produces sores. The good news is that they are highly preventable. To avoid infestation, bathe and shampoo regularly. Avoid wearing the same clothing for more than a day or two. Be sure to wash your clothes when they become soiled. Bed linens should also be changed and cleaned regularly. Finally, take care not to share combs, brushes, or hats with others, particularly if you know a person is suffering from head lice.

If you do contract head lice, they are highly treatable with medicated shampoos, creams, and ointments. Usually a single application of medicine works.

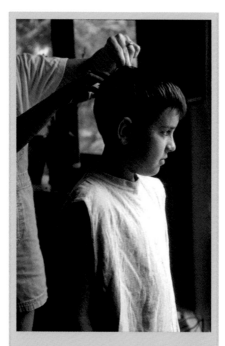

It's not unusual for children to get infected with lice, ringworm, and ticks, especially if they live in rural areas. Regular scalp examinations are a good way to catch lice infestations early.

In some cases, lice can spread to the eyebrows and eyelashes, which may require special treatment by a doctor. Other types of lice can affect different parts of the body, but frequent bathing and other precautionary measures can eliminate them.

Diseases Caused by Worms

Worms can be more dangerous to humans than lice because worms may live and multiply inside a person's body, unlike lice that exclusively live on the skin's surface. It is important to remind yourself that a parasitic worm is very different from most worms that you find in the garden. Common garden worms are usually beneficial to humans because they help break down soil and keep it nutritious for crops and other plant life.

While soil worms feed on the organic matter in dirt, parasitic worms feed off whomever they infest, be it a fish, animal, or person. There are many different kinds of parasitic worms. Virtually all begin by feeding on food and other nutrients stored within the host's body. If this supply dwindles as the worms produce and multiply, the parasites may begin to feed on blood and other body fluids. When this happens, the host may suffer from anemia, infections, and other health problems.

There are four principle methods of transmission, or ways in which people can become infected with parasitic worms. Worms spread to humans through water, food, insect bites, and contaminated soil.

Most parasitic worms that live in water can also live in food. That is because particles of food or waste material may wind up in water, creating a breeding ground for parasitic worms. Municipal treatment facilities carefully filter water and use certain chemicals, like chlorine, to rid water of parasites and other contaminants. Contracting worms from water is not common in the United States and other developed countries. Use of improperly tested well water, however, can lead to parasitic diseases. So can consuming water after a flood. Swimming in contaminated water is another way in which parasites can spread to humans. Some worms spread when a person eats contaminated food or accidentally swallows parasitic worms after touching a contaminated surface. These are the most common ways to get infected, particularly in the United States.

Schistosomiasis

In certain parts of Africa, South America, the Caribbean, China, the Middle East, and Southeast Asia, some types of snails harbor parasitic worms that cause a disease known as schistosomiasis. The parasites can penetrate the skin of a person who may be swimming or bathing in water where the snails live.

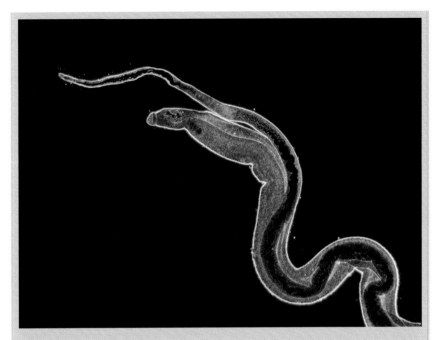

Once it infects a human, the worm *Schistosoma mansoni* lives in the blood vessels, shedding eggs that pass to the outside in human waste. Sometimes these eggs can become lodged in the liver and obstruct its blood flow.

Mild infections cause rash and flu-like symptoms. In more severe cases, the parasites can travel to the brain and spinal cord. Such an infection can even cause paralysis. Other major organs may also be damaged. Thankfully there are prescription drugs that can kill the worms and clear up the infestation.

Pinworms

One of the most prevalent infection-causing parasitic worms is the pinworm. This is a small white worm that resides in the human intestines. A sneaky worm, the pinworm leaves the intestines at night. Under the cover of darkness, females exit the body and lay eggs on the sleeping person's skin.

Young children are most often affected, as the worms often spread in child care centers, day camps, schools, and other places where close contact with victims might occur. Eggs laid on the skin can fall off and live for up to two weeks on clothes, bedding, and other objects. Usually a victim becomes infected after accidentally swallowing one or more of the microscopic eggs.

Because most pinworm infections are mild, many hosts for the worms show no symptoms, which can facilitate further spreading to other unsuspecting victims. Bad cases can lead to loss of appetite and difficulty sleeping, mostly due to the worm activity at night. Medicines taken over a two-week period can rid a person of the worms.

Household Pets and Worms

Dogs and cats commonly get tapeworms from fleas. The dog or cat, while grooming, may swallow an infected flea. Worms and eggs from the flea will then develop in the animal's intestinal tract. Aside from the presence of fleas, the clearest sign of infection is the presence of white or opaque rice-like specks near the pet's bottom. While usually not serious, worms should be treated because they can deplete the dog or cat of nutrients and can lead to stomach upset. Pet stores and even grocery stores usually carry wormers for pets, but veterinarian help should be sought, especially for severe cases or if the animal is very young or old.

Ascarids

The ascarid worm is similar to the pinworm and is by far the most common parasitic worm that bothers humans worldwide. In the United States, the presence of ascarids, small intestinal worms, usually occurs in rural areas of the Southeast. Among livestock, the animal most affected by ascarids, and parasitic worms in general, is the pig. That is because pigs eat close to the ground,

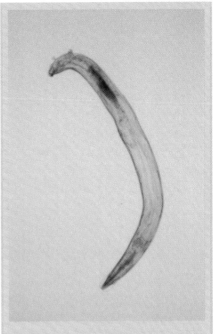

Most pinworm infections are mild and easily treated. Everyone in an affected household must be treated, and all clothes and linens washed to prevent reinfection.

may be fed contaminated food scraps, and spend a lot of time rolling around in dirt where the worms might reside.

Tapeworms and Roundworms

If humans eat contaminated meat that has not been properly cooked, they can become infected with parasitic worms. Two types of worms spread by

Taenia saginata (left), is a common tapeworm parasite in humans. It develops in cattle, infecting humans when they eat raw or undercooked beef. It causes hunger pains, weight loss, and weakness unless treated. The hookworm *Ancylostoma duodenale (right)* lives in the human intestines and can cause anemia and malnutrition, especially in children.

eating contaminated pork and beef are tapeworms and roundworms.

Tapeworms, which live in the small intestine of human hosts, can grow and reproduce for many years if left untreated. Some tapeworms may reach several feet in length. A single worm also can lay 50,000 eggs a day.

Trichinosis, caused by a roundworm, occurs when a person eats raw or undercooked pork infested by the parasitic worm. It causes everything from fever to heart problems. Trichinosis used to be common in the United States, but strict regulations on the way pigs are raised and butchered, and better recommendations for cooking pork, have nearly eliminated the problem.

Worms Carried in Insect Bites

Just as mosquitoes can transmit protozoa, these flying, biting vectors can also pass worms to humans. The disease called lymphatic filariasis (lim-FA-tick fil-uh-RYE-uh-sis) affects over 120 million people worldwide but does not occur in the United States. A threadlike worm that invades the lymphatic system causes the disease. In the United States, most parasitic worm infections happen after the ingestion of contaminated food and water, and not through insect bites.

Worms in Soil

The hookworm is one of the creepiest-looking intestinal parasites. The tip of a hookworm is a head with a giant open mouth full of

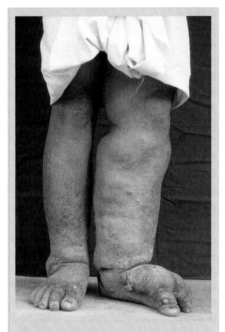

The legs of this man with lymphatic filariasis are severely swollen because his lymph nodes are not able to work properly. This disease is treatable, but some damage may be permanent.

teethlike structures that hook on to the walls of the human intestine, where the worm feeds. People can get the worm by walking barefoot in contaminated soil or by accidentally swallowing the worm. While hookworm disease has nearly been eliminated in the United States, worldwide it is said to affect 1 billion people, or around one-fifth of the entire human population. Drugs can kill the worm. In poor countries, however, medicine is not always available.

4 Understanding and Stopping the Parasite Cycle

Infection caused by parasites is highly treatable with prescription medications. Most humans do have at least one form of harmless amoeba in their intestines, but it does more good than harm by cleaning up excess waste. Parasites that can lead to diseases such as trichinosis or giardiasis clearly are not desirable guests. To prevent infestations before they happen, it helps to understand the life cycle of a typical parasite.

A Tapeworm's Life

Tapeworms are common parasites that may infest humans. They can spread in many different ways. Let's examine the life of a tapeworm now living in a big fish, and how it might spread and impact humans.

A fisherman on a camping trip catches the fish in a lake. He cooks it briefly over a camp stove and eats the fish for dinner. The tapeworm, having survived the brief cooking, grows and reproduces inside the unknowing fisherman. Human waste, containing tapeworm eggs, winds up in the soil and washes back into the lake. The eggs hatch and mature into adult tapeworms. A copepod, a type of crustacean, such as a small shrimp, swims by and eats the tapeworm. A small fish eats the shrimp. Later, an even bigger fish eats the small fish. At this point, the tapeworm has matured and multiplied, with the big fish now serving as host. A large animal, such as a human or a bear, catches the fish and the cycle begins all over again. Another camper could drink water from the lake and could also become infected and start another life cycle for the tapeworm.

Prevention and Control

As the tapeworm cycle demonstrates, parasites can pass to humans through water, food, and soil. An infected mosquito can also pass on a parasite through its bite. While there are many different kinds of parasites that multiply quickly, it is possible to stop the cycle from reaching humans.

Tap water in the United States must meet certain standards, so infection from municipal water is rare. If you are drinking untreated water, during a hike or camping trip, for example, or if you are traveling to countries without proper water treatment facilities, water still can be made safe to drink.

Boiling water for a minute or more usually kills any parasites that might be present. Iodine tablets,

Eating shellfish infected with enteroviruses can cause an outbreak of hepatitis A. The shellfish pick up the virus from sediment and water that have been polluted by sewage.

available at most pharmacies and sporting goods stores, also can kill parasites when the tablets are dissolved in water. Filters containing iodine can be used to protect against protozoa and worms.

When traveling outside of the United States to countries with known water problems, it is best to drink canned or bottled beverages. Avoid ice, as many parasites can survive below the freezing point of water. Boiled water drinks, like tea, are safer.

Even if you have not traveled much outside the country, you or someone you know probably has experienced a bout of food poisoning. A parasite, bacteria, or toxin in the food could have caused the problem. Since heat kills most of these microscopic, living organisms, chances are that the food was undercooked, raw, or allowed to stand for some time without being reheated before it is eaten. Fish, shellfish, and meat are especially problematic because they can contain parasites and their eggs.

Be sure to thoroughly cook foods as instructed on the packaging or in a cookbook. Fish, for example, requires less cooking time than pork, which must be heated to a certain internal temperature. When storing foods for transport, keep hot foods hot and cold foods cold using a thermos or some other special, protective container.

When eating abroad in countries with poor sanitation, avoid salads, other raw vegetable and fruit dishes, and unpasteurized milks and cheeses. Salads, for example, may have been washed with contaminated water. Also take care when purchasing food from street vendors. Make sure the food is fresh and heated before eating.

Are Sushi and Raw Meats Safe?

Given all of the health risks associated with raw fish and meats, it seems surprising that dishes like sushi, often made with raw fish and shellfish, and steak tartare, an uncooked meat dish, are popular in restaurants. Quality restaurants and markets hire trained professionals who can distinguish fresh meats and fish that are safe to eat raw from those that might be contaminated. When in doubt, select foods that have been cooked, as heating kills most parasites and germs.

Preventing Infection from Parasitic Insects and Vectors

The best way to prevent being bitten by a mosquito, flea, tick, or other insect associated with parasites is to avoid the biting bugs. Most disease-spreading mosquitoes are active at dawn or dusk, when temperatures are not too warm or cold. You may have even noticed more mosquitoes flying around outside your home during these times. It is then that they are likely to feed on unsuspecting hosts, like humans.

Fleas and ticks are a bit harder to track down. They can exist in certain rural areas, in tall brush or grass, or even in the fur of a family pet. Since it is impossible to completely avoid mosquitoes and other insects, sometimes other precautionary measures are necessary. Be sure to regularly wash the bedding of dogs and cats. Keep the animals well brushed and groomed. Bathe them when necessary. Cats do not always require baths, so check with your veterinarian first to ask about your specific pet.

When in outdoor areas where mosquitoes and parasitic insects are prevalent, wear protective clothing. Bugs cannot bite through most clothing, so anything that is covered will receive some protection. In rural places where there are a lot of fleas and ticks, pant legs can be tucked into socks, which will prevent fleas and ticks from touching your skin.

A number of insect repellents are available, even in grocery stores. Use them with the guidance of adults and only when protection from clothing and other methods are not enough. Also check the ingredients to see that they contain no harmful chemicals. Repellents containing permethrin, a natural substance made from chrysanthemum flowers, can last for several days when sprayed on shoes and clothing.

Parasites in the Twenty-First Century

A tourist reads under a mosquito net while camping in Queen Elizabeth National Park in Uganda.

Modern research, medicines, and other tools in the war against parasitic diseases help to keep parasites under control. Current problems, such as pollution, overpopulation, and climate change, however, often work in favor of parasites. The quality of water, food, and soil all suffer when under stresses that upset the natural balance. A fish weakened from bacteria present in a polluted lake, for example, would be more vulnerable to infestation by parasites. It is therefore important to address problems that affect the ecosystem.

If measures are taken to prevent the health threats posed by parasites, these seemingly lowly creatures may one day help us. Scientists are researching the survival skills of tapeworms and other parasites to improve drugs used to treat not only parasites, but also many kinds of illnesses. Parasites make good models because they can survive the harshest of environments, including the human intestines. The intestines normally eject a large percentage of vitamins and medicines taken orally, meaning that most of the good stuff goes to waste. Copying the tough nature of parasites, scientists hope to design drugs that can survive the environment of the intestines. If the project is successful, people will require less medicine in the future thanks to parasites.

Glossary

amebiasis   A food and waterborne disease caused by a parasitic protozoa.

apicomplexan   A type of parasitic protozoa; many of which cause disease.

arachnid   A spiderlike creature usually possessing eight legs and a body divided into two parts.

ciliate   A type of protozoa that propels itself with small hairs.

cryptosporidiosis   A waterborne disease caused by a parasitic protozoa.

cyclospora   A food and waterborne disease caused by a parasitic protozoa.

flagellate   Protozoa with tail-like extensions to assist in movement.

flea   A wingless insect that feeds on blood from a host.

giardiasis   A waterborne disease caused by a parasitic protozoa.

host   The organism that a parasite lives in or on.

malaria   A serious and widespread disease spread by mosquitoes carrying a parasitic protozoa.

parasite   An organism that lives in or on another living creature.

protozoa   Single-celled microscopic creatures that usually can move by themselves.

sarcodine   Protozoa with a toe-like appendage for locomotion; many have protective shells.

schistosomiasis   A disease caused by a parasitic worm.

tapeworm   A common form of parasitic worm that can grow several feet in length.

tick   An arachnid that feeds on blood from a host.

vector   An organism, such as an insect, that can spread disease.

worm   Animal with a soft, thin body without a backbone or ribs.

For More Information

Centers for Disease Control and Prevention
Mailstop C-14
1600 Clifton Road
Atlanta, GA 30333
(800) 311-3435
Web site: http://www.cdc.gov

National Institutes of Health
9000 Rockville Pike
Bethesda, MD 20892
(301) 496-4000
E-mail: NIHinfo@od.nih.gov
Web site: http://www.nih.gov

Owl Magazine
25 Boxwood Lane
Buffalo, NY 14227-2707
Web site: http://www.owlkids.com/owl

Science Made Simple Magazine
P.O. Box 503
Voorhees, NJ 08043
E-mail: questions@sciencemadesimple.com
Web site: http://www.sciencemadesimple.com

The U.S. Department of Health and Human Services
200 Independence Avenue SW
Washington, DC 20201
(202) 619-0257 or (877) 696-6775
Web site: http://www.hhs.gov

The World Health Organization
Avenue Appia 20
1211 Geneva 27
Switzerland
+41 22 791 2111
E-mail: info@who.int
Web site: http://www.who.int/en

Web Sites

Due to the changing nature of Internet links, the Rosen Publishing Group, Inc., has developed an online list of Web sites related to the subject of this book. This site is updated regularly. Please use this link to access the list:

http://www.rosenlinks.com/germ/para

For Further Reading

Berger, Melvin. *Flies Taste with Their Feet: Weird Facts About Insects*. New York: Scholastic Inc., 1997.

Berger, Melvin. *Germs Make Me Sick*. New York: HarperCollins Children's Books, 1995.

Dunn, Gary. *Insect Life Cycle Studies: Entymology*. Collingdale, PA: Diane Publishing Co., 1998.

Haslam, Andrew. *Insects: The Hands-on Approach to Science*. Chanhassen, MN: Creative Publishing International, Inc., 2000.

Hooper, Meredith. *The Drop in My Drink: The Story of Water on Our Planet*. New York: Viking Penguin, 1998.

Miller, Sarah Swan. *Will You Sting Me? Will You Bite?: The Truth about Some Scary Looking Insects*. Owings Mills, MD: Stemmer House Publishers, Inc., 2001.

Patten, Barbara J. *Food Safety: Food for Good Health*. Vero Beach, FL: Rourke Publishing, LLC, 1995.

Snodgrass, Mary Ellen. *Environmental Awareness: Water Pollution*. Marco, FL: Bancroft-Sage Publishing Incorporated, 1991.

Stone, Lynn. *Amazing Insects*. Vero Beach, FL: Rourke Publishing, LLC, 2001.

Bibliography

Drexler, Madeline. *Secret Agents: The Menace of Emerging Infections*. Washington, DC: Joseph Henry Press, 2002.

Dye, Lee. "Sticking Around: Tapeworm Could Hold Key to Getting Meds to Stay in Digestive System." http://www.ABCNews.go.com/sections/scitech/DyeHard/dyehard030312.html. Retrieved March 12, 2003.

Sharma, Rajenda. *The Family Encyclopedia of Health*. Boston: Element Books Limited, 1998.

Simon, Hilda. *Partners, Guests and Parasites: Coexistence in Nature*. New York: Viking Penguin, 1970.

World Book Online Americas Edition. Chicago: World Book Inc., 2003.

Index

About the Author

Jennifer Viegas is a reporter for Discovery Channel Online News and is a features columnist for Knight Ridder Newspapers. She has worked as a journalist for ABC News, PBS, the *Washington Post,* the *Christian Science Monitor,* and other media. Jennifer also helped to write two heart-healthy cookbooks for *Cooking Light.*

Photo Credits

Cover, pp. 13, 15 © Gary D. Gaugler/Photo Researchers, Inc.; pp. 3,4,9,12,20,22, 28, 33,36, 40–48 courtesy of Public Health Image Library/Centers for Disease Control and Prevention; p. 6 © David M. Phillips/ Photo Researchers, Inc.; pp. 8, 16, 19 (lower right), 23, 27 © Eye of Science/Photo Researchers, Inc.; p. 10 © Educational Images/Custom Medical Stock Photo; p. 19 (center) © Sinclair Stammers/Photo Researchers, Inc.; p. 19 (upper left) © London School of Hygiene/ SPL/Custom Medical Stock Photo; p. 21 © V. Steger/ Photo Researchers, Inc.; p. 24 © Custom Medical Stock Photo; p. 29 © J. Siebert/Custom Medical Stock Photo; p. 30 (left and right) © CNRI/ Photo Researchers, Inc.; p. 31 © SPL/Custom Medical Stock Photo; p. 35 © Pablo Corral V/Corbis; p. 38 © Ray Wood/ Panos Pictures.

Designer: Thomas Forget; Editor: Jake Goldberg; Photo Researcher: Sherri Liberman